CONTENTS

SPINE-TINGLING GHOST TALES 4

Z HIGH STREET.................. 5

SANJAY GANDHI
NATIONAL PARK................. 8

KELLIE'S CASTLE............... 10

CHAONEI NO. 81............... 12

JERUK PURUT CEMETERY...... 16

PENANG WAR MUSEUM......... 18

CHANGI BEACH................ 20

THE FORBIDDEN CITY 22

BUILDING 2283,
KADENA AIR BASE 26

CLARK AIR BASE HOSPITAL..... 28

MAP 29
GLOSSARY 30
FIND OUT MORE......... 31
INDEX 32

Spine-tingling ghost tales

Ghost stories come from every corner of the world. Asia is the world's largest continent, and it is rich with **haunted** places. Looking for creepy graveyards? Want to hear about piercing shrieks in the night coming from **abandoned** buildings? You can find them in Asia. No one knows if ghosts are real. But one thing is certain: These ghostly tales from Asia will send a tingle up your spine!

haunted having mysterious events happen often, possibly due to visits from ghosts

abandoned deserted or no longer used

Bhangarh Fort is known as one of the most haunted places in India.

FAMOUS GHOST STORIES FROM ASIA

by Jillian L. Harvey

Raintree is an imprint of Capstone Global Library Limited, a company incorporated in England and Wales having its registered office at 264 Banbury Road, Oxford, OX2 7DY – Registered company number: 6695582

www.raintree.co.uk
myorders@raintree.co.uk

Edited by Carrie Braulick Sheely
Designed by Kyle Grenz
Original illustrations © Capstone Global Library Limited 2019
Picture research by Svetlana Zhurkin
Production by Kathy McColley
Originated by Capstone Global Library Ltd
Printed and bound in India

ISBN 978 1 4747 5960 1
22 21 20 19 18
10 9 8 7 6 5 4 3 2 1

British Library Cataloguing in Publication Data
A full catalogue record for this book is available from the British Library.

Acknowledgements
We would like to thank the following for permission to reproduce photographs: Dreamstime: Arik Chan, 20–21; Getty Images: Hindustan Times/Prasad Gori, 8, The Montifraulo Collection, 6–7; iStockphoto: simongurney, 28; Newscom: Kyodo, 27, Pictures From History, 22, Sipa USA/Sipa Asia/Yu Yi, 14, Zuma Press/Donal Husni, 16–17; Shutterstock: Arina P Habich, cover (back), Azman AlKurauwi, 10–11, dikobraziy (map), 5, 8, 10, 12, 16, 18, 20, 22, 26, 28, 29, EQRoy, 26, GolubaPhoto, 9, Joe Prachatree, cover (front), Kush Rathod, 4, Mahod84, 23, Mohd Nasri Bin Mohd Zain, 19, Sergii Rudiuk, 24–25; Wikimedia: ChingMing, 5, Daniel Case, 13. Design Elements by Shutterstock.

2 High Street

LOCATION: HONG KONG, CHINA

Hong Kong, China, is home to many ghost stories. One of its most haunted places stands at 2 High Street. The building is more than 125 years old, and it has housed its share of dreadful events. Some people believe these events led to the reports of hauntings.

British nurses first lived at 2 High Street after it was built in 1892. These nurses worked at a nearby hospital. During World War II (1939–1945) the building became a **psychiatric** hospital. Female patients with mental disabilities lived there. In 1961 another hospital opened, and 10 years later the hospital at 2 High Street shut its doors. For nearly 30 years no one lived in the building. But was it really empty?

psychiatric related to a branch of medicine that studies the mind, emotions and behaviour

Soon after it closed, people started reporting ghostly sightings at 2 High Street. Some people said headless **poltergeists** wandered the corridors at night. People heard unexplained screams echoing from within the walls. The building's best-known tale is of a ghostly figure dressed in traditional Chinese clothing. If it meets eyes with the living, it bursts into flames.

the hospital at 2 High Street in 1900

poltergeist noisy ghost

In 1998 workers built the Sai Ying Pun Community Centre at 2 High Street. The L-shaped front of the old building remains. Today the centre is bustling with visitors all day. But the building's ghost stories are alive and well. Once the sun sets, only the brave dare step inside.

FACT

After it was abandoned, the old hospital at 2 High Street became known as the "High Street Haunted House".

Sanjay Gandhi National Park

LOCATION: MUMBAI, INDIA

Dangers lurk in the dark woods of India's Sanjay Gandhi National Park. This park borders the country's largest city, Mumbai. Leopards creep among towering trees. Snakes slither under leaves. But it's the park's reported ghosts that may offer its creepiest encounters.

Wild animals in the park have taken the lives of several people. Some people believe the **spirits** of these victims wander the park. The park's most commonly seen ghost is a female dressed in white. She is hitch-hiking. At night she stands beside the road waiting for a car to approach. When a driver pulls over, she asks for a lift. But before getting in the car, she vanishes.

spirit ghost

Park visitors report other **paranormal** activity. People say they've heard voices when no one is around. They report the uncomfortable feeling of being watched. The park closes during the evening. If the stories are true, maybe it's good that visitors leave before darkness settles.

paranormal having to do with an event that has no scientific explanation

Many versions of the vanishing hitch-hiker

People tell tales of vanishing ghostly hitch-hikers throughout the world. No one knows how the **legends** began. Many of the stories go back hundreds of years. European stories tell of travellers riding on horseback who met lifelike ghosts wanting to join them. American stories from the 1870s tell of hitch-hiking ghosts approaching travellers in carriages and wagons.

No matter the story, two parts usually stay the same. The hitch-hiker is almost always female and she always vanishes suddenly. Sometimes the ghost disappears following its request for a lift, but usually it disappears during the journey. In some stories the hitch-hiker leaves behind an item such as a jacket.

legend story passed down through the years that may not be completely true

Kellie's Castle

LOCATION: BATU GAJAH, MALAYSIA

In Batu Gajah, Malaysia, winding roads lead to an old, lonely castle at the top of a hill. Kellie's Castle is named after Scottish businessman and farmer William Kellie Smith. Smith began building the castle in the early 1900s. He wanted it to look like his previous home in Scotland. He planned for it to have unique and grand features, such as Malaysia's first lift. But he never got the chance to finish the project. In the late 1920s Smith died suddenly. His wife left Malaysia with their children. The castle remains unfinished today. But it may not be completely abandoned. According to local stories, several ghosts have made it their home.

Over the years the castle's ghost stories attracted visitors. Some of these visitors have left convinced the terrifying tales are true. People have reported hearing unexplained screams and voices echo through the castle. Some visitors have reported seeing Smith's ghost wandering the corridors. Others claim to have spotted the ghost of a young girl with curly hair dressed in white in one of the rooms. Some people believe it is the ghost of Smith's daughter, Helen. One witness reported seeing the ghost of a castle guard with no legs. Other reports include a feeling of being watched and hearing unexplained footsteps.

FACT

Several workers employed by Smith to build the castle died of Spanish flu. Some people believe their ghosts also haunt the castle.

Chaonei No. 81

Vines creep up the sides of an empty brick mansion in Beijing, China. Oddly shaped pieces of broken glass sit in window openings. The mansion's walls inside are covered in **graffiti**. Leaves and branches litter the floor. No one has lived in the home for more than 50 years. But some locals believe the house may not really be empty.

Ownership records for Chaonei No. 81 are incomplete. Legend says that an officer fighting in the Chinese Civil War (1927–1949) once lived there. After defeat in 1949, he escaped to Taiwan. He left his wife behind. She was heartbroken and lonely. In her despair, she ended her own life. Locals claim her ghost has haunted the house ever since.

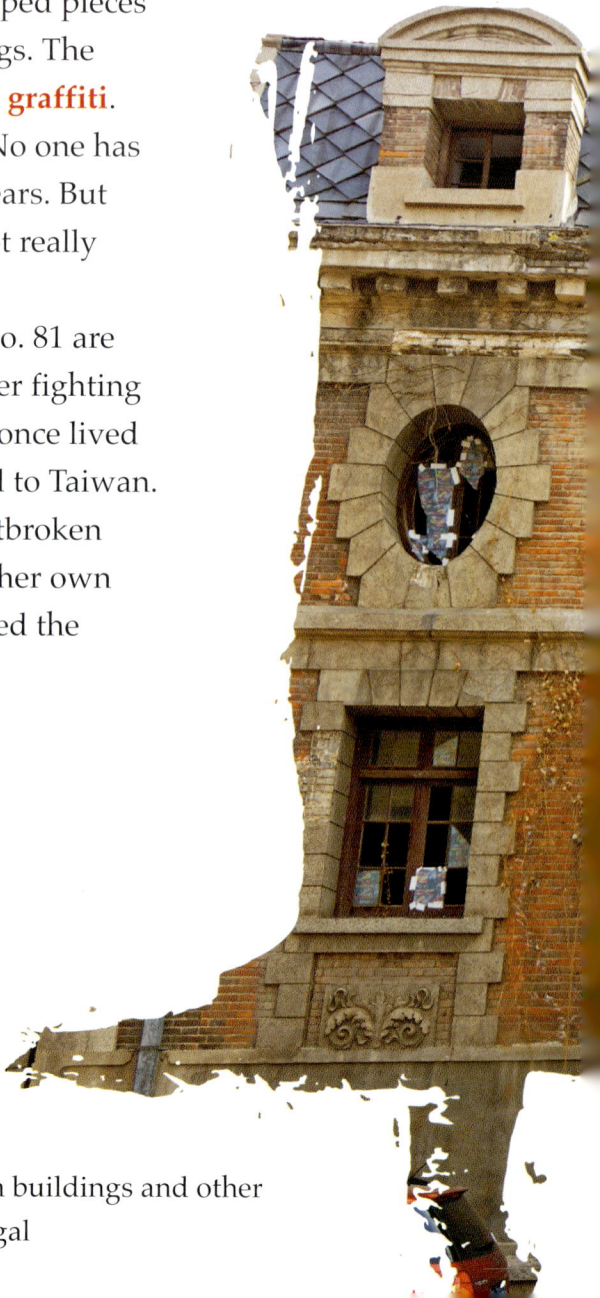

graffiti pictures or words painted on buildings and other public spaces; most graffiti is illegal

Chaonei No. 81 was the setting for the 2014 film *The House That Never Dies* and its 2017 sequel. Since the first film's release, daring thrill seekers have come to the house hoping to find out for themselves if it's haunted.

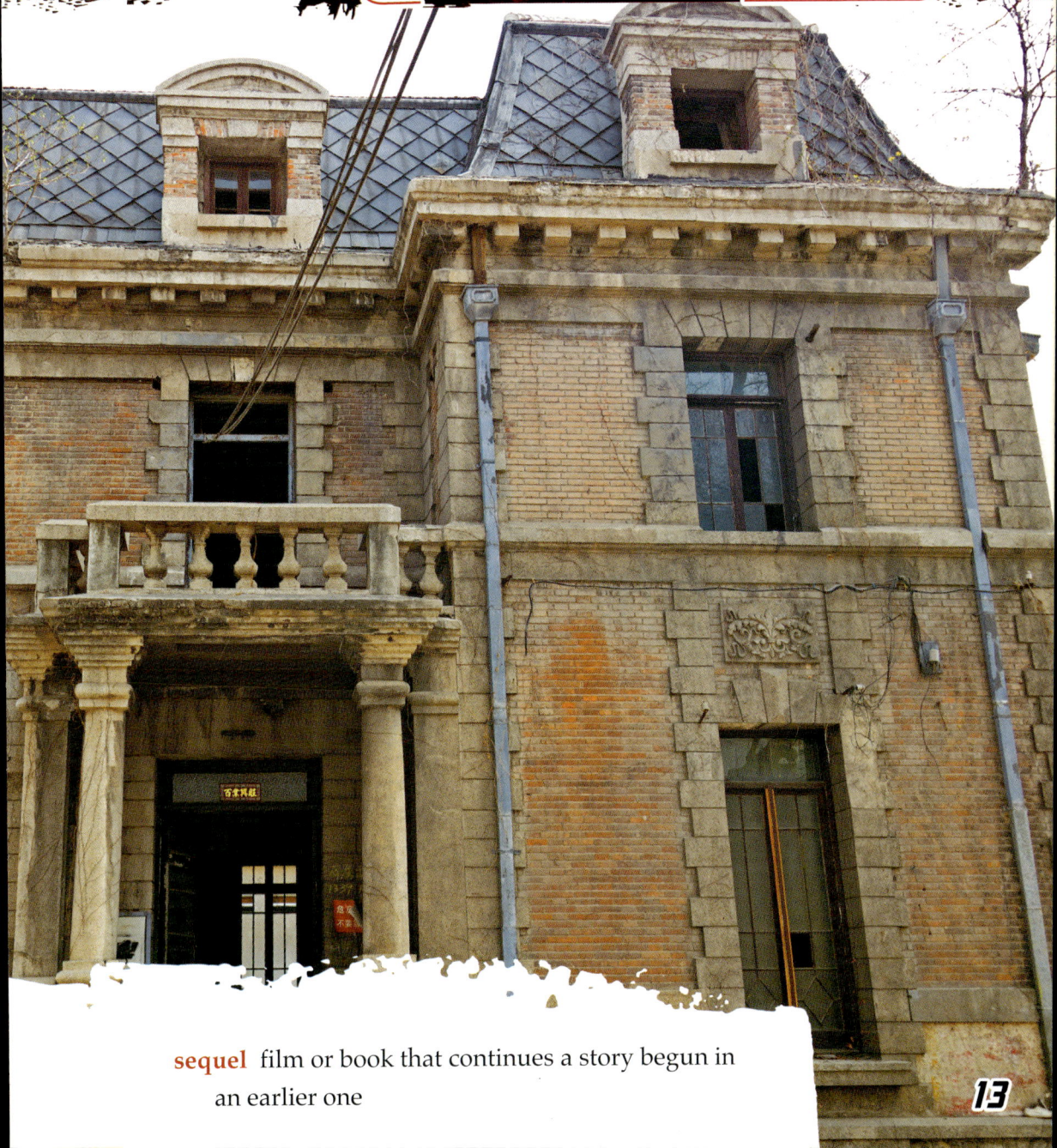

sequel film or book that continues a story begun in an earlier one

People have reported many paranormal activities at the mansion. During thunderstorms loud screams are said to echo throughout the house. Some people report an uneasy feeling when passing by the home. Visitors say that the air at the front door is much cooler than it is in surrounding areas. Paranormal experts believe that large drops in temperature may be a sign that ghosts are present.

The city of Beijing has the mansion on a historic building **preservation** list. This might be one of the reasons why it has remained empty for so long. It can only be repaired, not torn down, which would be very expensive. The stories about its ghosts might keep people away too.

Stories of mysterious disappearances

Rumours tell of people disappearing from Chaonei No. 81. According to one story, the Chinese government built the mansion as a gift to the Catholic Church. A British priest oversaw the construction of the home around 1910. One day he suddenly went missing. Investigators later discovered a tunnel that stretched from the **crypt** in the building's basement to the nearby neighbourhood of Dashanzi. The priest was never found. Did he die in the crypt? Did he escape to Dashanzi? More than 100 years later, his disappearance remains a mystery.

Another story tells of a group of builders who were working on a neighbouring home's basement. Late one summer night in 2001, the men discovered a thin wall that separated the home from Chaonei No. 81. They decided to break through the wall. It's said they were never seen again.

preservation protecting something so that it stays in its
original condition

crypt underground chamber

Jeruk Purut Cemetery

LOCATION: JAKARTA, INDONESIA

Weather-beaten headstones rise from the earth. Dead bodies rest below the grass. Few places are spookier than cemeteries. Jeruk Purut Cemetery in Jakarta, Indonesia, is no exception.

Jeruk Purut's best-known ghost is that of an old pastor. People say that this headless figure roams the cemetery carrying his head. The ghost of a large black dog follows closely behind him. Some people believe the pastor is searching for his grave. According to legend, he appears on Friday nights, only when visitors are in groups of odd-numbered people.

The headless pastor's search for his grave site may never end. It is believed his grave is actually located in Tanah Kusir Cemetery in Bintaro, South Jakarta.

A cemetery caretaker has given ghost tours at Jeruk Purut. He said that once when he was walking around the cemetery, he could not put his foot down on the ground. He claimed a ghost of a child kept lifting it up. He also talked of a hairy ghost that shows itself near a stream on the property.

FACT

The 2006 Indonesian horror film *Hantu Jeruk Purut* is based on the story of the headless pastor ghost.

Penang War Museum

LOCATION: PENANG, MALAYSIA

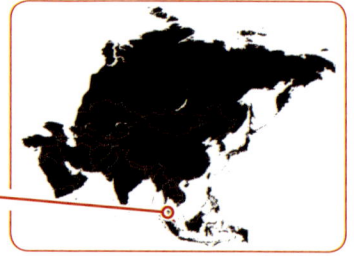

High on a hill in Penang, Malaysia, sits one of Asia's most haunted structures. The British built the fort in the 1930s. During World War II, Japanese forces overtook it. The Japanese used the fort as a prisoner-of-war camp. The fort's haunted history has earned it the name "Ghost Hill".

According to legend, a merciless leader called Tadashi Suzuki helped run the prison. He carried a **samurai** sword and used it to kill prisoners. Both prisoners and other soldiers feared him. After the war the building was empty for more than 50 years.

In 2002 the building became the Penang War Museum. Museum staff claim to have seen ghosts roaming the property. A night guard once saw a ghost holding a rifle with a bayonet in one hand. In the other hand was a samurai sword. Was it the ghost of Suzuki?

samurai skilled Japanese warrior who served one master or leader; the samurai fought between 500 and 1877

Today people from around the world come to the Penang War Museum. Some of these visitors are paranormal enthusiasts. Ghost hunters who have visited say they've heard voices of ghosts. One says he even had a short conversation with a ghost. He said he asked what the ghost wanted him to do. The ghost replied, "to die".

Changi Beach

LOCATION: CHANGI, SINGAPORE

White sand stretches along the coast of Changi Beach in Singapore. By day it is a peaceful place. But by night, it might be absolutely terrifying.

During World War II, a horrific war crime happened at Changi Beach. Japanese forces wanted to kill all Chinese **civilians** in Singapore who they believed to be anti-Japanese. On 20 February 1942, a merciless Japanese firing squad killed 66 Chinese men at the water's edge. Their bodies were buried nearby.

FACT

After the war some Japanese soldiers found guilty of war crimes were also executed at Changi Beach.

civilian person who is not in the military

Today some people believe the ghosts of the killed civilians haunt the beach. Visitors have heard unexplained cries and screams. They've seen headless ghosts walking along the shore. These ghosts hold their heads in their arms. Visitors to the beach houses have reported feeling as if they are being watched. They have also said that the beach house doors open and shut on their own.

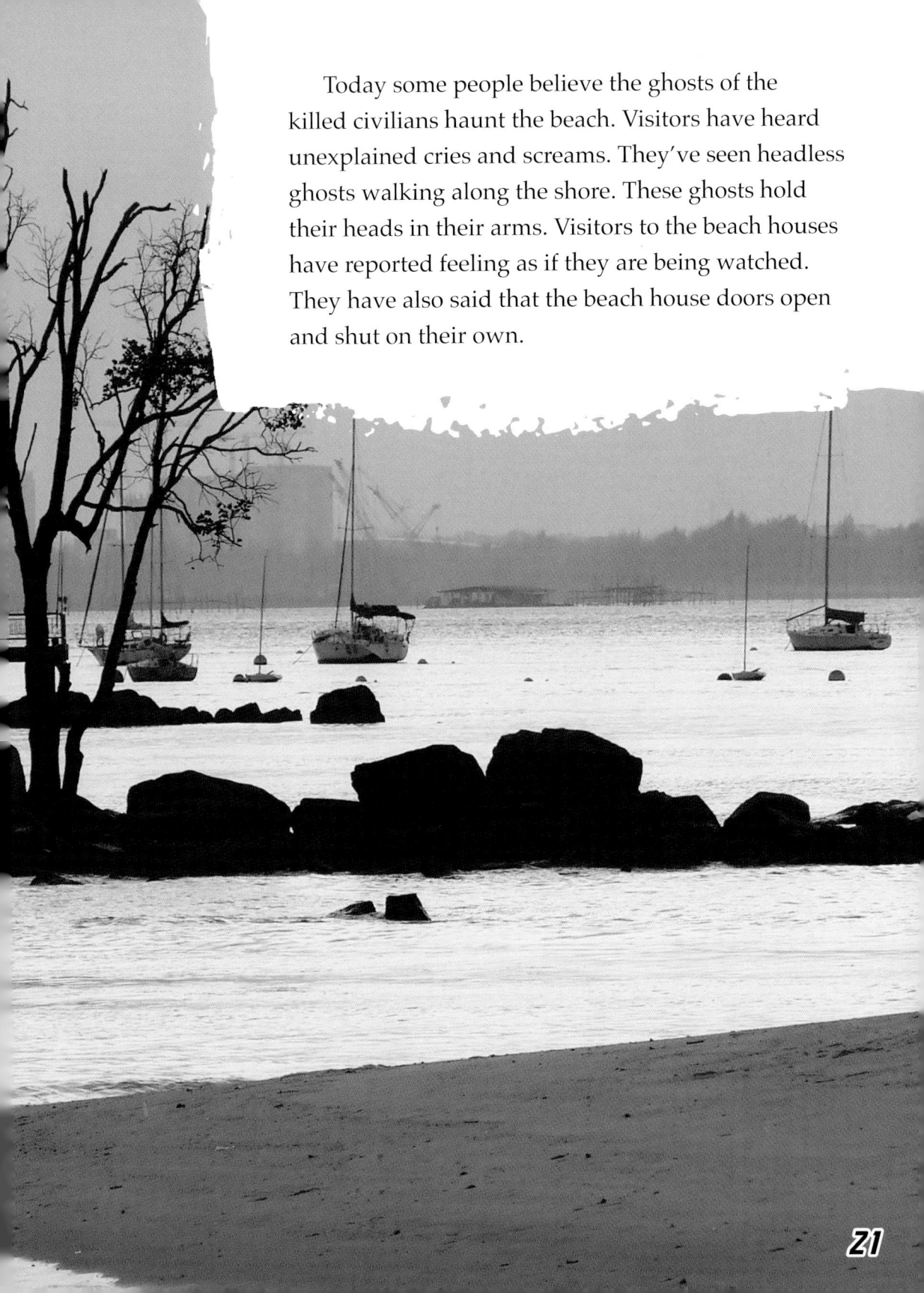

The Forbidden City

LOCATION: BEIJING, CHINA

In the heart of Beijing, China, stands a palace complex known as the Forbidden City. Many betrayals and deaths have happened since it was built. Today people link these events to the paranormal experiences visitors report there.

Builders finished the Forbidden City in 1420. It was a palace for emperors. Until the early 1900s, 24 emperors ruled China from the palace. Emperor Yongle was the first to live there. He was a cruel leader, and he treated Chinese citizens poorly. In 1421 Yongle ordered his soldiers to kill thousands of people. He thought the people could reveal his secrets. Most of these victims were women.

Emperor Yongle

Some people say ghosts of these victims haunt the palace today. According to a soldier nicknamed Fat Fu, in 1995 two guards were on patrol. They met a woman with long hair in a black dress. They called to her, but she did not respond and ran away. They chased her. When they caught up to her, she turned to them. The men quickly saw that she had no face!

Other female ghosts may haunt the palace.
People say a ghostly woman dressed in white
roams the grounds. She is always crying.
People have also heard women's sorrowful
cries at night.

Witnesses report other unexplained happenings at the site. At night guards have heard ghostly music playing. They have also seen ghostly animals running around the vast grounds. Visitors have heard unexplained sounds of sword fighting. Some people have even reported seeing blood mysteriously appear.

In the 1940s the palace was opened to the public. Today the Forbidden City complex is home to the Palace Museum. The museum's director believes the ghost stories are just tales. Museum operators have recently opened areas to visitors that had previously been closed. They hope this will help limit talk about closed areas being haunted.

FACT

The Forbidden City is one of the world's most popular tourist sites. Nearly 16.7 million people visited it in 2017.

Building 2283, Kadena Air Base

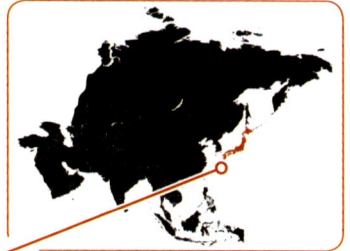

LOCATION: OKINAWA, JAPAN

Kadena Air Base is a US Air Force base on the island of Okinawa, Japan. The US military captured the airfield that became Kadena Air Base in World War II. Workers originally built Building 2283 as a single-family home on the base for officers.

At first the house was peaceful. Then in the 1970s a husband is said to have murdered his wife in the home. Years later it's believed another murder occurred. Afterwards base officials stopped housing military families there. The Air Force then used the house for storage for several years. In the late 2000s, workers tore down the building.

Before being destroyed, the home was well known for ghost sightings. People at the base were curious about the home and sometimes explored the building's interior. Some people reported seeing the ghost of a woman washing her hair in the sink. The home's lights flickered on and off and its taps ran and stopped for no apparent reason. Some people witnessed the ghost of a samurai riding on horseback through the home. The building is said to be across the street from a samurai's tomb.

Today many people believe the site remains haunted. A day-care centre borders the land where the building once stood. Day-care staff have said that children claim to talk to other children on the old building's site. But the day-care staff have never seen any other children!

Clark Air Base hospital

LOCATION: ANGELES, PHILIPPINES

Desperate cries call from the **morgue**. A ghost with a skeleton face wanders around the reception. These are just some of the paranormal activities reported at the Clark Air Base hospital in Angeles, Philippines.

Clark Air Base was built in the early 1900s for US military forces. Its hospital saw heavy use during the Vietnam War (1959–1975). In 1991 the volcanic Mount Pinatubo erupted and blanketed the base in 3.7 metres (12 feet) of ash. Afterwards, the Americans chose to leave.

After its abandonment, people began spreading tales of ghostly events at the hospital. Some people said ghosts threw objects at them. A former security guard said he heard shouts coming from the hospital's morgue. "Help me, help me. I don't want to die," the voices said.

In 2009 team members of Ghost Hunters International visited the site. They heard unexplained footsteps. One person saw a white figure that quickly vanished. Could it have been the ghost of a fallen soldier?

morgue place where dead bodies are kept until they are identified or released for burial

Map: Haunted locations of Asia

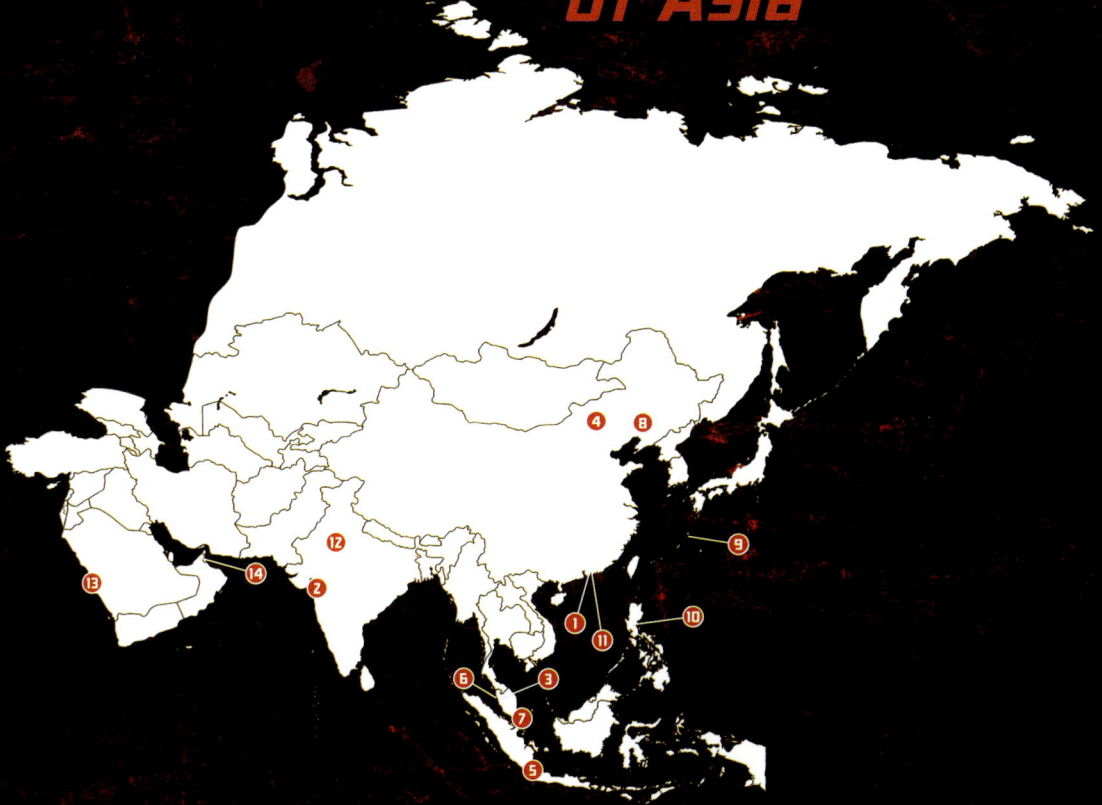

1. Z High Street · Hong Kong, China

2. Sanjay Gandhi National Park · Mumbai, India

3. Kellie's Castle · Batu Gajah, Malaysia

4. Chaonei No. 81 · Beijing, China

5. Jeruk Purut Cemetery · Jakarta, Indonesia

6. Penang War Museum · Penang, Malaysia

7. Changi Beach, Changi, Singapore

8. The Forbidden City · Beijing, China

9. Building ZZ83, Kadena Air Base · Okinawa, Japan

10. Clark Air Base hospital · Angeles, Philippines

11. Tat Tak School · Hong Kong, China

12. Bhangarh Fort · Rajasthan, India

13. Haunted House of Jeddah · Jeddah, Saudi Arabia

14. Al Qasimi Palace · Ras Al Khaimah, United Arab Emirates

GLOSSARY

abandoned deserted or no longer used

civilian person who is not in the military

crypt underground chamber

graffiti pictures or words painted on buildings and other public spaces; most graffiti is illegal

haunted having mysterious events happen often, possibly due to visits from ghosts

legend story passed down through the years that may not be completely true

morgue place where dead bodies are kept until they are identified or released for burial

paranormal having to do with an event that has no scientific explanation

poltergeist noisy ghost

preservation protecting something so that it stays in its original condition

psychiatric related to a branch of medicine that studies the mind, emotions and behaviour

samurai skilled Japanese warrior who served one master or leader; the samurai fought between 500 and 1877

sequel film or book that continues a story begun in an earlier one

spirit ghost

FIND OUT MORE

BOOKS

Chinese Myths and Legends (All About Myths), Anita Ganeri (Raintree, 2013)

Ghosts and Haunted Houses (Solving Mysteries with Science), Jane Bingham (Raintree, 2013)

Japan (Countries Around the World), Patrick Catel (Raintree, 2013)

Living Through the Vietnam War, Cath Senker (Raintree, 2013)

Paranormal Handbook to Ghosts, Poltergeists and Haunted Houses (Paranormal Handbooks), Sean McCollum (Raintree, 2016)

WEBSITES

www.bbc.co.uk/cbbc/watch/hetty-feathers-creepy-and-ghostly-stories
Listen to some hair-raising ghost stories!

www.dkfindout.com/uk/more-find-out/festivals-and-holidays/hungry-ghost-festival
Learn about the hungry ghost festival celebrated in many Asian countries.

INDEX

2 High Street 5, 6–7

Changi Beach 20–21
Chaonei No. 81 12, 13, 15
Chinese Civil War 12
Clark Air Base hospital 28

Emperor Yongle 22

Fat Fu 23
Forbidden City 22–25

hitch-hiking ghost stories 8, 9
hospitals 5, 7, 28

Japanese forces 18, 20
Jeruk Purut Cemetery 16–17

Kadena Air Base 26–27
Kellie's Castle 10–11

Mount Pinatubo 28

Penang War Museum 18–19
poltergeists 6

Sai Ying Pun Community Centre 7
Sanjay Gandhi National Park 8–9
Smith, William Kellie 10–11
Spanish flu 11
Suzuki, Tadashi 18

Vietnam War 28

World War II 5, 18, 20, 26